SHORT CATECHISM
OF MARY

D1571103

THE IMMACULATE CONCEPTION — Mary's privilege of freedom from original sin shows that she is the chosen daughter of the Father, the faithful Spouse of the Spirit, and the devoted Mother of the Son.

SHORT CATECHISM OF MARY

By

Cardinal Charles Journet

**WITH TWO ADDITIONAL APPENDICES:
MARY IN THE LITURGY
AND POPULAR PRAYERS TO MARY**

Illustrated

CATHOLIC BOOK PUBLISHING CORP.
New Jersey

NIHIL OBSTAT: James T. O'Connor, S.T.D.
Censor Librorum

IMPRIMATUR: Patrick J. Sheridan
Vicar General, Archdiocese of New York

This book was originally published in French under the title *Petit Catechisme de la Sainte Vierge* by Editions Saint-Augustin, Saint-Maurice (Switzerland). The English translation is by Anthony M. Buono.

(T-50)

All creatures have been created to serve God, and God has reserved to Himself the means by which to use each of them.

Mary, who we are told is essentially the hand-maid, served God. Why then would not God make use of her?

What Mary accomplished, isn't this what God accomplished through her?

Paul Claudel
The Rose and the Rosary

CONTENTS

Chapter 4

THE LIFE OF THE BLESSED VIRGIN

Chapter 5

OUR LOVE FOR THE BLESSED VIRGIN

Appendix 1

MARY IN THE LITURGY

Appendix 2
POPULAR PRAYERS TO MARY

PREFACE

THE last chapter of the *Constitution on the Church* by the Second Vatican Council, without intending to propose a complete doctrine of the Blessed Virgin Mary, recalls her role in the mystery of Christ and the Church: her presence in the Old Testament as the Mother of the expected Messiah, her virginal motherhood, her presence in the life of Jesus, her immaculate conception, and her assumption into heaven.

By reason of the part Mary played in the drama of the redemption of the world, she became our Mother in the order of grace; in heaven she continues to intercede for us as Advocate, Auxiliatrix, Adjutrix, and Mediatrix. She is the firstfruits of the future Church and the sign of hope of the present Church.

Pope Paul VI declared: "It is the first time that an Ecumenical Council presents such a vast synthesis of the Catholic teaching concerning the place that Mary most holy occupies in the mystery of Christ and the Church."

To solemnize this event, the Sovereign Pontiff adds: "To the glory of the Blessed Virgin and for our consolation, *we proclaim that Mary most holy is Mother of the Church,* that is, of the whole People of God, both of the faithful and of the shepherds, who invoke her as their most loving Mother. We desire that henceforth the Blessed Virgin may be more honored and invoked under this most sweet title by the whole Christian people."

At the foot of the Cross, the Blessed Virgin united herself more closely than any other person to her Son's desire to save the whole world. She intercedes—more insistently than at Cana—that this desire may be fulfilled in all human beings, so that all those who do not refuse may be *saved.* In this sense, she is *the Mother of all human beings,* whether they know it or not.

But for those who are openly members of the Mystical Body whose Head is Christ, her intercession is colored by a new flame. She makes supplication so that, in accord with the power of each, they may be in some slight way—through Christ, with Christ, and in Christ—not only *saved* but also *saviors* of other human beings. In this precise sense, Mary is invoked as *Mother of the Church.*

MOTHER OF THE CHURCH — On the first Pentecost, the Church was born when the Holy Spirit descended upon the Apostles with Mary in their midst in the Upper Room (Acts 2:1-4).

14

Chapter 1

MARY, MOTHER OF THE CHURCH

Summary

- It is God's exceptional love for Mary
  that is at the basis
  of her Divine Motherhood.

  (qq. 1-3)

- The Blessed Virgin has truly the right
  to the title of Mother of God.

  (qq. 4-7)

- At what moment did she become,
  freely and willingly, the Mother of God?

  (qq. 8-10)

- Just as the Incarnation is the beginning
  of all the graces that Jesus received,
  so the Divine Motherhood is the beginning
  of all the graces that Mary received.

  (q. 11)

The Love of God
Beginning of the Divine Motherhood

1. Who is the creature most loved by God?

The creature most loved by God is the Blessed Virgin.

2. How did God manifest this to us?

By choosing her to be the Mother of the Child Jesus. It is of Mary that the Gospel says that she "gave birth to Jesus Who is called the Messiah" (Matthew 1:16).

3. Did God have to love the Blessed Virgin a great deal in order to ask her to be the Mother of the Child Jesus?

Yes. This is the most sacred task that God could confer upon a creature. God has therefore loved the Blessed Virgin more than all the Angels and all the Saints.

Mary, True Mother of God

4. **Can the Blessed Mother be called the Mother of God?**

Yes, because she is the Mother of Jesus, Who is God. On seeing her, Elizabeth exclaimed: "And why am I so greatly favored that the Mother of my Lord should visit me?" (Luke 1:43).

5. **Why did Christians begin to call Mary the Mother of God?**

In order to answer those who asserted: "Jesus is not God! So Mary, the Mother of Jesus, is not the Mother of God!"

6. **When did this begin?**

This began in the East already around the 3rd century. In the 4th century, St. Gregory Nazianzen wrote: "If anyone does not believe that the Blessed [Virgin] Mary is the Mother of God, that person is separated from the Deity!"

7. Which life did the Blessed Virgin give Jesus?

The Blessed Virgin did not give Jesus the *Divine Life* that He possesses eternally in heaven. She gave Him the *human life* that He came to seek on earth.

The Moment of the Incarnation

8. When did the Blessed Virgin become the Mother of God?

The Blessed Virgin became the Mother of God on the day of the Annunciation, when God sent the Archangel Gabriel to her at Nazareth, to tell her that she was to become the Mother of the Savior.

9. What response did the Blessed Virgin make to the Archangel Gabriel?

She said: "I am the servant of the Lord. Let it be done to me according to your word" (Luke 1:38).

10. Did the Blessed Virgin then understand how much God loved her?

Yes, for she said: "Henceforth all generations will call me blessed. The Mighty One *has done great things for me*" (Luke 1:48-49).

The Divine Motherhood
Cause of All the Privileges of Mary

11. Did the Blessed Virgin receive other graces?

Yes. But the grace of being the Mother of God is the cause of all the others.

MARY GIVES BIRTH TO JESUS — Mary gave birth to her firstborn Son. She wrapped Him in swaddling clothes and laid Him in a manger (Luke 2:7).

Chapter 2

THE MOST HOLY VIRGIN

Summary

- The Blessed Virgin carried out
  her mission as Mother of God
  in a most holy manner.
  She was, according to Revelation,
  the worthy Mother of God.   (qq. 12-15)

- Understood in this way,
  the idea of the Divine Motherhood entails
  the idea of a fullness of grace.   (qq. 16-20)

- It excludes the presence in Mary's soul
  of all personal sin
  both mortal and venial.   (qq. 21-24)

- It also excludes the original sin
  to which she would have to be subject
  as a child of Adam.
  Because of her Immaculate Conception
  the imperfection, stain, and defilement of
    original sin
  never touched her soul.   (qq. 25-28)

- Even the consequences of original sin
  were spared her body
  after her death
  because of her Assumption.   (qq. 29-34)

The Worthy Mother of God

12. How did the Blessed Virgin carry out her mission as the Mother of God?

The Blessed Virgin carried out her mission as the Mother of God in a most holy manner. She was the most worthy Mother of God.

13. What is meant by "worthy Mother of God"?

This phrase means: (1) Mary understood the meaning of the Angel's message; (2) she freely and fully consented to what God expected of her; and (3) from then on she reached the heights of her exalted mission, a radiant but heart-rending task that surpassed simple human powers.

14. Is all this contained in St. Luke's account?

Yes, if we give it all its depth; that is, if we read it (1) while believing in the mystery of the Incarnation and (2) while noticing the great delicacy, respect, and love with which God addresses Mary.

15. Did the Fathers of the Church understand that Mary was a worthy Mother of God?

Yes. St. Augustine wrote that Mary was the Mother of Jesus "even more with her soul than with her body."

Fullness of Grace

16. What first gift did Mary receive to be the worthy Mother of God?

According to the Evangelist, God bestowed on Mary the gift of being the Mother of Jesus by a *miracle*. This is affirmed twice: in St. Luke (1:34-37) and in St. Matthew (1:20). This is why we say that she is a Virgin and Mother. It is the privilege of Mary's *virginal Motherhood*.

17. What other gifts did she receive to be the worthy Mother of God?

God gave Mary the *fullness of grace*, that is, of holiness; that is why we call her the Blessed Virgin.

18. Could the Blessed Virgin have been the worthy Mother of God without being full of grace?

No! This becomes impossible when one understands all that is meant by the phrase *worthy Mother of God*.

19. Did the Angel Gabriel know that the Blessed Virgin was full of holiness?

Yes. He announced to her that she was marked by grace (Luke 1:28) and that she had found grace with God (Luke 1:28).

20. Did Elizabeth, her cousin, know that the Blessed Virgin was full of holiness?

Yes. She tells Mary that she is blessed among all women, that she is the Mother of the Lord, and that she is blessed for having believed the Angel (Luke 1:42-45).

Exemption from All Personal Sin

21. Did the Blessed Virgin commit at least some sins?

No, she never committed any sin, mortal or venial.

22. How do we know that the Blessed Virgin never committed any sin?

If she had committed even the slightest sin, she could not truly be called full of grace, neither would she have been the worthy Mother of God.

23. Did not the Blessed Virgin act indiscreetly in asking for the miracle of Cana?

No, for Jesus heard her request and advanced the hour of His manifestation on her account.

He said to her: "Woman, why should this be of any concern to Me? My hour has not yet come" (John 2:4). This meant: "Woman, these things have very little importance! My hour to manifest Myself and to perform a miracle has not yet come. Nevertheless, I will grant your request."

24. When did Jesus speak to His Mother in a solemn manner by addressing her as "Woman"?

He addressed her in this way twice, when He was going to act externally in the fullness of His Divine power.

He did so at Cana, when His hour was beginning, and so He performed the miracle
that she requested.

He also did so at Calvary, when His hour
was ending, and so He gave her to us as our
Mother (John 19:26).

Immaculate Conception

**25. Even though the Blessed Virgin did not
herself commit any sin, didn't she at least
inherit the stain of original sin?**

No! In order for her to be truly full of grace
and the worthy Mother of God, God *preserved* her from the stain of original sin; she
did not need to be *purified* from it as we do
through Baptism.

**26. Did the Blessed Virgin herself achieve re-
demption through the prayer of Jesus on
the Cross?**

Yes. It is because of the prayer that Jesus
would *later* make on the Cross that God *in
advance* preserved the Blessed Virgin from
the original stain.

27. What do we call this privilege of the Blessed Virgin?

We call it the Immaculate Conception. This means that at her conception—that is, at the moment when her soul was created and united with her body—she was Immaculate, preserved from the original stain.

28. Does the Bible say anything that announces the Immaculate Conception?

Yes. The Bible recounts that the devil caused the first woman, who had been immaculate, to sin.

Nevertheless, after this sin, God did not abandon our first parents. He promised them vindication, and He announced that in their turn the Woman and her Offspring would vanquish the devil (Genesis 3:15).

The sacred writer of the Book of Revelation explains that the Woman who vanquishes the devil is above all the Blessed Virgin; her Offspring is above all her Son Jesus (Revelation 12:1-5).

The Assumption

29. What takes place at our death as a consequence of original sin?

Our body decomposes, and it will not rise before the end of the world.

30. What took place, on the contrary, at the death of Jesus?

The body of Jesus did not decompose. It rose again and ascended into heaven on the day of the Ascension.

31. What took place at the death of the Blessed Virgin?

The body of Mary did not decompose. Jesus raised it up and took it to heaven on the day of the Assumption.

32. Is the revelation of the Assumption based on Scripture?

Yes. It is based above all on two viewpoints, one of St. Paul and the other of his disciple St. Luke.

33. What is the teaching of St. Paul about the Resurrection of Christ and that of Christians?

St. Paul teaches that God, who has raised and glorified Christ will raise and glorify Christ's faithful as well. Christ, Who is without sin, is raised and glorified at once. But the faithful, because they are touched by sin, can be raised and glorified only at the end of the world, when sin and death will be fully vanquished.

34. When would the Blessed Virgin have been raised and glorified?

The Blessed Virgin would have been raised and glorified only at the end of the world, like us, if she had been touched by sin. But because, as St. Luke teaches, she was free of all sin and truly full of grace, she was raised and glorified immediately after death—like Christ.

MARY AT THE CROSS — Mary stood silently near the Cross of her suffering Son and heard Him give her into John's care before He died. This made her our Mother also (John 19:26-27).

Chapter 3

MARY, MOTHER OF ALL HUMAN BEINGS

Summary

- Just as Eve is responsible for our misery,
  Mary is responsible for our salvation.
  She is our Mother according to grace.
  (qq. 35-36)

- She intervenes on earth in the acquisition of
    grace—
  the first time in a more remote manner
  by accepting to be the Mother of the Savior.
  (qq. 37-38)

- The second time she does so
  in a more proximate manner
  by participating in the redemptive sacrifice,
  becoming Reparatrix and Coredemptrix with
    Jesus.
  (qq. 39-44)

- In heaven she intervenes
  in the distribution of graces,
  as Dispensatrix or Mediatrix of all graces.
  (qq. 45-46)

Mary, Our Mother according to Grace

35. Can we compare Eve and Mary? *

Yes. Eve, who listened to the devil and dis-
obeyed God, had the greatest part after
Adam in bringing about the misery of all
human beings. Mary, who listened to the
Angel and obeyed God, had the greatest part
after Jesus in bringing about the salvation of
all human beings.

St. Irenaeus wrote around the year 200:
"Just as Eve, having Adam as spouse but still
a virgin, was through her disobedience

---

* Pope Pius XII in his *Encyclical on the Queenship of Mary* declared: "Mary in the work of redemption was by God's will joined
with Jesus Christ, the cause of salvation, in much the same way as
Eve was joined with Adam, the cause of death. Hence it can be said
that the work of our salvation was brought about by a 'restoration'
(St. Irenaeus) in which the human race, just as it was doomed to
death by a virgin, was saved by a Virgin.

"Moreover, she was chosen to be the Mother of Christ in order
to have part with Him in the redemption of the human race. She it
was, who, free from all stain of personal or original sin, always
most closely united with her Son, offered Him up to the Eternal
Father on Calvary, along with the sacrifice of her own claims as His
Mother and of her own Mother love, thus acting as a new Eve on
behalf of all Adam's children, ruined by his unhappy fall.

"From this we conclude that just as Christ, the new Adam, is our
King not only because He is the Son of God but also because he is
our Redeemer, so also in a somewhat similar manner the Blessed
Virgin is Queen not only as Mother of God but also because she
was associated as the second Eve with the new Adam."—*Trans.*

the cause of death for herself and the whole human race, so Mary, destined for a spouse but still a virgin, was through her obedience the cause of salvation for herself and the whole human race."

Tertullian wrote around 210: "Eve believed the serpent and Mary believed Gabriel; where the credulity of Eve results in sin, the faith of Mary results in reparation."

36. Who willed that the Blessed Virgin should have so great a part in the salvation of human beings?

Jesus. It was He who willed to await the response of the Blessed Virgin to the Angel before coming to earth to save human beings.

Mary Gives Us Jesus, Source of Grace

37. When did the Blessed Virgin become for the first time the Mother of all human beings in the order of grace?

At the Annunciation, when she became the Mother of Jesus, Author and Source of grace for all human beings.

38. **Did the Blessed Virgin already have a great love for all human beings?**

Yes. She was happy to know that Jesus would come to save human beings from their sins (Matthew 1:21), and she was ready to suffer much for our salvation (Luke 2:35).

Mary Coredemptrix

39. **After the birth of Jesus, did the Blessed Virgin still do very great things for the salvation of human beings?**

Yes. She united herself with all the sufferings of Jesus during His life and during His Death.

40. **When did the Blessed Virgin become for the second time the Mother of all human beings in the order of grace?**

On Calvary, when she prayed that the sacrifice of Jesus might bring grace to all human beings.

41. **At that moment, did Jesus think of the great sufferings of His Mother?**

Yes. He thought of the great sufferings of His Mother and He united them to those that He Himself endured to save us.

42. **What difference is there between the sufferings of Jesus and those of the Blessed Virgin?**

The sufferings of Jesus, Who is God, have an infinite value: they are *redemptive.*

The most holy sufferings of the Blessed Virgin and of Christians have only a finite value: they are solely *coredemptive.*

43. **Is not Jesus our unique Savior, our unique Mediator, our unique Redeemer?**

Yes. Jesus, Who is God, is our unique Savior: it is He Who first saves the Blessed Virgin and then sends her to help us.

Jesus, Who is God, is the unique Mediator Who can *redeem us,* that is, can give the heavenly Father an *infinite* compensation for our sins. He is, according to St. Paul, the "one Mediator . . . Who gave Himself *as a ransom* for all" (1 Timothy 2:5-6). The Blessed Virgin, who is the holiest of creatures, could give the heavenly Father only the holiest of *finite* prayers.

Thus, Jesus is our unique Redeemer; and the Blessed Virgin is our supreme Coredemptrix. Jesus, Who is God, is our unique Mediator in the line of *infinite redemption;* and the Blessed Virgin, who is a creature, is our supreme mediatrix in the line of *finite coredemption.*

44. Did Jesus speak of the Blessed Virgin when He was on the Cross?

Yes. He gave the Blessed Virgin as Mother to St. John and, through him, to all human beings: "When Jesus saw His Mother and the disciple whom He loved standing beside her, He said to His Mother, 'Woman, behold, your son.' Then He said to the disciple, 'Behold, your mother'" (John 19:26-27).

Mary, Mediatrix of All Graces

45. Is the Blessed Virgin concerned about us from heaven on high?

Yes. She continues to intercede for the world with her Son Jesus. In the name of the coredemptive prayer that she offered at the foot of the Cross, she obtains all the graces of salvation that unceasingly reach human beings.

46. Did God have need of the Blessed Virgin?

God never has need of any creature. However, in order that we might know how much He loved the world, He willed to choose the Blessed Virgin and to associate her closely with His birth and His sacrifice and in the dispensation of His graces.

JESUS APPEARS TO MARY — At dawn on Easter Sunday Jesus rose from the dead and tradition tells us He appeared first to His Mother. She thus shared in the joy and glory of His triumph.

Chapter 4

THE LIFE OF THE BLESSED VIRGIN

Summary

- The Blessed Virgin was descended
  from the line of David
  and spent her childhood
  in the Temple.

  (qq. 47-49)

- The Gospel speaks a great deal
  about the Blessed Virgin
  with respect to the Childhood of Jesus.

  (qq. 50-56)

- But it speaks about her even more
  with respect to the life of Jesus,
  even though the vocation of the Blessed Virgin
  was that of the hidden life.

  (qq. 57-59)

- Some time after the coming of the Holy Spirit
  on Pentecost,
  the Blessed Virgin died
  and was taken body and soul into heaven.

  (qq. 60-61)

The Childhood of the Blessed Virgin

47. What do the Sacred Books say about the ancestors of Mary?

The Sacred Books tell us that Mary descended from David, for Jesus was "descended from David according to the flesh" (Romans 1:3).

48. What are the first two feasts of the Blessed Virgin?

The Feast of the Immaculate Conception on December 8 and the Feast of the Birth of Mary on September 8.

49. In addition to what the Sacred Books say about Mary, do we know other things about her childhood?

We know that her mother was St. Ann and her father was St. Joachim and that she was brought to the Temple of Jerusalem to be raised there. The Church celebrates the Presentation of Mary in the Temple on November 21.

The Blessed Virgin in the Gospel During the Childhood of Jesus

50. At what moment does the Gospel begin to speak about the Blessed Virgin?

At the moment when the mystery of the Incarnation is about to be accomplished and when the Angel announces to her that by a miracle she is to become the Mother of the Savior (Luke 1:26-38): this is the Feast of the Annunciation on March 25.

The Blessed Virgin responds to the Angel: "Behold, I am the servant of the Lord. Let it be done to me according to your word" (Luke 1:38).

51. Whom does the Blessed Virgin go first to visit?

The Blessed Virgin goes first to visit her cousin, St. Elizabeth: this is the Feast of the Visitation on July 2. Elizabeth says to Mary: "Blessed are you among women, and blessed is the fruit of your womb. And why am I so greatly favored that the Mother of my Lord should visit me?" (Luke 1:42-43). It is then that the Blessed Virgin sings the canticle of thanksgiving known as the *Magnificat* ("My Soul Proclaims the Greatness") (Luke 1:46-55).

52. Was St. Joseph the true father of the Child Jesus?

No. The Child Jesus had as His real father the heavenly Father. St. Joseph was only His protector and His father before the law (Matthew 1:18-25).

53. Did Jesus have real brothers and sisters?

No. Jesus had no real brothers and sisters. St. James, his closest relative (Galatians 1:7), had a different mother (Mark 15:40). In the Gospel, the phrase "brothers and sisters of Jesus" signifies cousins and relatives of Jesus.

54. What did the Blessed Virgin do after the birth of Jesus?

The Blessed Virgin took Him to the Temple of Jerusalem to consecrate Him to God (Luke 2:22-38): this is the Feast of the Presentation of the Child Jesus in the Temple and the Purification of the Blessed Virgin on February 2. It is then that the aged Simeon took the Child Jesus into his arms and sang the Canticle of farewell known as the

Nunc Dimittis ("Now You Dismiss"). He foretells that the Child will be a sign of contradiction and "a sword will pierce" Mary herself (Luke 2:29-35).

55. What do the Blessed Virgin and St. Joseph do after the visit of the Magi at Bethlehem?

After the visit of the Magi at Bethlehem, the Blessed Virgin and St. Joseph flee into Egypt to escape the massacre of the infants ordered by Herod (Matthew 2:13-14).

56. What is the last event of the Childhood of Jesus recounted in the Gospel?

The Gospel tells us that when the Child Jesus was twelve years old, His parents lost Him at Jerusalem and rediscovered Him in the Temple. He said to them: "Why were you searching for Me? Did you not know that I must be in My Father's house?" But they did not yet understand how or why their hearts had been broken by the demands of their Son's Divine mission (Luke 2:41-50).

The Blessed Virgin During the Public Life of Jesus

57. Is the Blessed Virgin spoken about in connection with the Public Life of Jesus?

Yes, especially in two places. At the beginning of His Public Life, Jesus performs His first miracle at Cana as a result of the prayer of the Blessed Virgin (John 2:1-11). At the end, at the moment of His death on the Cross, Jesus gives the Blessed Virgin as Mother to St. John (John 19:26-27).

58. Is the Blessed Virgin spoken about any place else in the Gospel?

St. Mark recounts that in a house surrounded by a crowd, Jesus is accused by His enemies of being a demoniac.

"When His relatives heard about this, they went out to take charge of Him, saying, 'He has gone out of His mind.'. . . A crowd was sitting around Him, and they said, 'Behold, Your mother and Your brothers [and Your sisters] are outside asking for You.' He replied, 'Who are My Mother and [My] brothers?'

"Then, looking around at those who were near Him, He said, 'Behold, My Mother and My brothers. For whoever does the will of God is My brother and sister and Mother'" (Mark 3:21, 31-35).

Jesus does not deny the ties of *temporal* kinship between husbands and wives, parents and children. But He establishes over and beyond these the bonds of a new kinship, which is *spiritual,* and which effaces the other by its splendor as the sun effaces the light of lamps.

Henceforth, the Blessed Virgin must no longer act visibly on the plane of *temporal* kinship to defend Jesus and comfort Him but only invisibly on the plane of *spiritual* kinship to unite herself to His zeal for the things of God and to His redemptive sufferings. But on this plane as on the other, she will remain the first of all.

St. Luke recounts that on another occasion, a woman with a great heart took up the defense of Jesus and cried out: "'Blessed is the womb that bore You and the breasts that nursed You.' Jesus replied, 'Blessed, rather, are those who hear the word of God and obey it'" (Luke 11:27-28). Listen to the word of God and obey it—that was the very thing this magnanimous woman was doing! And Jesus made it clear that this was precisely what He loved most in His Mother.

59. Was the role of the Blessed Virgin public like that of the Apostles?

No. The role of the Blessed Virgin was to watch over the Hidden Life of Jesus and to accompany Him at His death. Then to pray and suffer in silence for the Church: this is a hidden role.

Death of the Blessed Virgin

60. Is the Blessed Virgin spoken about after Jesus' departure into heaven?

In the Book of the Acts of the Apostles, it is said that after the Ascension the eleven, Apostles withdrew to the Upper Room and "were constantly engaged in prayer, together with the women and Mary the Mother of Jesus, and with His brothers"(1:14). It is there that the Holy Spirit came to visit them on the day of Pentecost (Acts, 2:1)—but with opposite effects.

For the Apostles, princes of the grandeur of the hierarchy, Pentecost is a beginning, a departure toward the conquest of space and time. For the Blessed Virgin, all hidden in the grandeurs of sanctity, Pentecost is an end, the announcement of her departure for heaven.

61. **When do we celebrate the death, resurrection, and ascent into heaven of the Blessed Virgin?**

We celebrate the death, resurrection, and ascent into heaven of the Blessed Virgin toward the end of summer on the day of the Assumption, August 15.

MARY CROWNED QUEEN OF HEAVEN — Mary is Queen of heaven and earth. She shares in the glory of her Son just as she shared in His sufferings on earth through which He redeemed the world.

Chapter 5

OUR LOVE FOR THE BLESSED VIRGIN

Summary

● We must love the Blessed Virgin
because she is the Mother of God
and the Mother of all human beings.

(qq. 62-63)

● The love of the Blessed Virgin
leads to the love of God
and its depths.

(qq. 64-69)

● It is expressed in the ordinary prayer
of the "Hail Mary"
and in our Marian prayers.

(qq. 70-72)

● For true servants of the Blessed Virgin,
this love is a pledge of predestination.

(qq. 73-74)

The Blessed Virgin Is Worthy of Our Love

62. Who teaches us to love the Blessed Virgin?

God does. For it is He Who has loved her more than all other creatures.

63. After love for God, what should be our greatest love?

After the love of *adoration* reserved for God, Creator of the universe and Author of our salvation, our greatest love should be the love of *veneration* that we have for the Blessed Virgin, the Mother of God and our Mother.

64. Can we love the Blessed Virgin too much?

No. The more we love, in the Blessed Virgin, what she has been for Jesus, the more we will become like Jesus. But we will never love her as much as Jesus did.

True Love for the Blessed Virgin Is Inseparable from Love for God

65. Does love for the Blessed Virgin lead away from love for God?

No. If the Blessed Virgin is a path to God, the more we love God, the more will we love the Blessed Virgin. Hence, true love for the Blessed Virgin must always increase.

66. Can we not love God without loving the Blessed Virgin?

No. It is impossible to love God without loving the Blessed Virgin once we know that she is truly the Mother of God.

67. Is it necessary to think expressly of the Blessed Virgin every time we think of God?

No. The Blessed Virgin, even if she is not named, is happy about every prayer that rises to God.

68. Does true devotion to the Blessed Virgin run counter to the adoration due to Jesus?

Not at all. In fact, we see that wherever devotion to Mary is given up, faith in the Divinity of Christ tends to disappear.

69. What request should we often make to the Blessed Virgin?

We must often ask the Blessed Virgin to take us under her mantle and make us understand and love—somewhat as she understood and loved—the mysteries of the life of Jesus, His joys, His sufferings, and His triumphs.

The Prayer of the "Hail Mary"

70. When was the "Hail Mary" introduced into the Liturgy?

The first part, which is in the Gospel, appeared in an Entrance Antiphon of the Mass around the 6th century. It began to spread among the faithful beginning with the 13th century.

The second part ("Holy Mary...") , whose elements preexisted in a separated state, was put together beginning with 1400 and became current among the faithful a little after 1500.

71. How should we say the "Hail Mary"?

We must say the "Hail Mary" not only with the lips but with the heart as well; not only for oneself but for all human beings; and while remembering that the salvation of the world began with this prayer.

We must say the "Hail Mary" as it was begun the first time on earth by the Angel at the Annunciation and continued by Elizabeth at the Visitation. (See p. 67.)

The Principal Marian Prayers

72. What are the dates of the principal prayers that we address to the Blessed Virgin?

These prayers are for the most part by unknown authors. They bear witness to the devotion of all the subsequent Christian centuries. They appeared spontaneously like the various flowers in each season.

In the 3rd century, there appeared the Greek text of the prayer *Sub Tuum Praesidium* ("We Fly to Your Protection"— p. 67). This is a popular prayer to ask for the intercession of the Mother of God in our needs and dangers.

In the 10th century, the hymn *Ave Maris Stella* ("Hail, Thou Star of Ocean"—p. 67) implores her who as our Mother hears our prayers and will in turn be heard by her Son. The antiphon *Regina Caeli Laetare* ("Queen of Heaven, Rejoice"—p. 68) sings of the joy of the Blessed Virgin on the day of Easter.

In the 11th century, the antiphon *Alma Redemptoris Mater* ("Mother Benign of Our Redeeming Lord"—p. 68) is an address on the part of the sinful people striving to rise to the Virgin who is accessible despite being so high, that she brought the light of day to her Creator. The antiphon *Salve Regina* ("Hail Holy Queen"—p. 68) supplicates her who is the sweetness of our life to show us her Son Jesus after our exile in this valley of tears.

In the 12th century, the antiphon *Ave Regina Caelorum* ("Hail, O Queen of Heaven"—p. 69) celebrates the glory of the Queen of heaven, who gave birth to Christ, the Light of the world.

In the 14th century, the *Stabat Mater Dolorosa* ("At the Cross Her Station Keeping"—p. 69) is the great heart-shattering hymn of the sufferings of Compassion endured by the Blessed Virgin at the foot of the Cross.

In the 15th century, there comes into being our version of the *Litany of the Blessed Virgin* (p. 71), Mother of Christ and Virgin for the world, a Helper for us and a Queen for the Angels. At the same time, the *Rosary* receives its actual form, in which we ask the Blessed Virgin to unite with her own and immerse in the joys, sorrows, and victories of her Son: our poor sorrows, so that they may not be bitter; our poor victories, so that they may always be magnanimous. (See p. 72.) At the same epoch, there appeared the touching popular prayer of the *Memorare* ("Remember . . ."—p. 80).

True Love for the Blessed Virgin Opens the Gates of Heaven

73. How can we especially please the Blessed Virgin?

By purifying our hearts from sin; and by imitating her faith and her love, her obedience and her greatness of soul: for to love is to imitate.

74. Is the Blessed Virgin powerful enough to obtain the salvation of her true servants?

Yes. The Blessed Virgin is powerful enough to obtain the salvation of her true servants, that is, those who from the bottom of their hearts without ceasing ask her to help them to rise from sin, to live in the light of the Gospel, and to die in the love of God.

APPENDICES

The two Appendices are not part of Cardinal Journet's work. They have been added as a further aid to those who make use of this Catechism.—*Trans.*

MARY'S ASSUMPTION — After her death Mary is assumed body and soul into heaven. The Assumption is one of the greatest Feasts of Mary celebrated in the Liturgy.

APPENDIX 1:

MARY IN THE LITURGY

Summary

- The Liturgy is the public worship of the Church
  that enables us to worship God
  and obtain graces for our salvation.

  (qq. 75-76)

- The Church renders devotion to Mary
  by celebrating 14 major Marian Feasts.

  (qq. 77-82)

- Mary is also mentioned daily at Mass,
  commemorated on Saturday in Ordinary Time,
  and given liturgical honor during the month
  of May.

  (qq.83-86)

- Mary is present at each Eucharist
  in her Divine and Risen Son
  and as our Model, Intercessor, and Mother.

  (qq. 87-91)

- Devotion to Mary
  glorifies the Blessed Trinity,
  gives us a better understanding of Mary's
    part in salvation,
  and makes the Mysteries of Christ become
    present to us
  in their relationship with Mary.

  (qq. 92-96)

Liturgical Devotion to Mary

75. What is the Liturgy?

The Liturgy is the public worship of the
Church (Head and members) in the Mass
and other Sacraments, the Liturgy of the
Hours and the Liturgical Year, and the other
Sacramentals.

What does the Liturgy do?

The Liturgy makes present Christ's Paschal
Mystery (His Life, Death, and Resurrection),
enabling us to render fitting worship to God
and to obtain the graces Christ gained for all
human beings.

The Liturgical Feasts of Mary

77. Why does the Church render liturgical devotion to Mary?

The Church renders liturgical devotion to
Mary because Mary is joined by an insepa-
rable bond to the saving work of her Son.

78. How many feasts of Mary are in the liturgical calendar in the United States?

There are sixteen feasts of Mary celebrated
in the United States.

79. Which are the five feasts of low rank known as Optional Memorials?

Our Lady of Lourdes (Feb. 11), Our Lady of Fatima (May 13), Our Lady of Mount Carmel (July 16), Dedication of St. Mary Major (Aug. 5), and the Most Holy Name of Mary (Sept. 12).

80. Which are the five feasts of moderate rank known as Obligatory Memorials?

Immaculate Heart of Mary (Saturday after the Solemnity of the Sacred Heart of Jesus), Queenship of Mary (Aug. 22), Our Lady of Sorrows (Sept. 15), Our Lady of the Rosary (Oct. 7), and Presentation of Mary (Nov. 21).

81. Which are the six feasts of high rank known as Feasts or Solemnities?

Solemnity of the Motherhood of Mary (Jan. 1), Feast of the Visitation (May 31), Solemnity of the Assumption (Aug. 15), Feast of the Birth of Mary (Sept. 8), Solemnity of the Immaculate Conception (Dec. 8), and Feast of Our Lady of Guadalupe (Dec. 12).

82. In what other feasts does Mary also have an important role?

Mary has an important role in the Solemnity of the Annunciation (Mar. 25) and the Feast of the Presentation of our Lord (Feb. 2) as well as other feasts of her Son.

Other Ways of Showing Liturgical Devotion to Mary

83. Is Mary mentioned daily in the Ordinary of the Mass?

Yes. Mary is mentioned every day in the Introductory Rites at the "I Confess," in the Liturgy of the Word at the Nicene Creed, and in the Liturgy of the Eucharist at all ten Eucharistic Prayers.

84. Is Mary commemorated in the Common of the Mass?

Yes. There are six special Marian formulas in the Common of the Mass that can be used at different times.

85. Is Mary commemorated on Saturdays in Ordinary Time?

Yes. Many of the Saturdays in Ordinary Time (outside Advent, Christmas Time, Lent, and Easter Time) are open days when the Mass of the Blessed Virgin on Saturday may be celebrated.

86. Is Mary given liturgical honor during May?

Yes. The entire month of May is dedicated to Mary, and many churches have a daily recitation of the Rosary in public or some prayers in honor of Mary, including the rite of crowning her image.

Mary's Presence in the Celebration of the Eucharist

87. Why is Mary present in the Eucharist?

Mary cooperated in a singular way in the Savior's work of restoring grace to souls and is a mother to us in the order of grace. Because of this close connection with Christ and us, Mary could not be absent from our celebration of the Eucharist.

88. How does Mary's presence in the Eucharist differ from Christ's?

The consecration at Mass effects the Real Presence of the Christ of Glory in the act of His Sacrifice under the appearances of bread and wine, with His Body and Blood, Soul and Divinity. Nothing of the kind is true in Mary's humanity.

89. How is Mary present in the Eucharist?

Mary is present in the Risen Christ, Who took from her His Body and Blood that are offered in the Eucharistic Sacrifice.

90. How else is Mary present?

Mary is also present because she was associated with her Son in the work of salvation that is being re-presented in the Eucharist.

91. In what capacity is Mary present in the Eucharist?

Mary is present as our Model, our Intercessor, and our Mother.

Benefits of Liturgical Devotion to Mary

92. Whom do we honor and praise when we show devotion to Mary?

We honor and praise God the Father for the wisdom of His designs manifested in Mary.

93. Whom do we get to know and love better through the devotion tendered to Mary?

We get to know and love better Jesus Christ, the Son of God.

94. What is acknowledged and proclaimed in the liturgical devotion to Mary?

We acknowledge and proclaim the action of the Holy Spirit in Mary and in the Church.

95. What is each Marian liturgical celebration intended to give us?

It is intended to give us a better understanding of Mary's part in our salvation—a true catechesis of Mary.

96. What happens as the Liturgy honors Mary over the course of a year?

The Mysteries of Christ become present to us in their relationship with Mary.

MARY'S INTERCESSION — At Cana, Mary obtained Jesus' first miracle. In heaven, she now intercedes for us with her Son, especially in answer to our prayers.

APPENDIX 2

POPULAR PRAYERS TO MARY

HAIL MARY

HAIL Mary,
full of grace,
the Lord is with you.
Blessed are you among
women
and blessed is the fruit
of your womb, Jesus.

Holy Mary,
Mother of God,
pray for us sinners,
now and at the hour of
our death.

WE FLY TO YOUR PATRONAGE

WE fly to your pa-
tronage,
O holy Mother of God;
despise not our petitions
in our necessities,

but deliver us always
from all dangers,
O glorious and blessed
Virgin.

HAIL, THOU STAR OF OCEAN

HAIL, thou star of
ocean,
God's own Mother blest,
Ever sinless Virgin,
Gate of heavenly rest.

Oh! by Gabriel's Ave,
Uttered long ago,
Eva's name reversing,
'Stablish peace below.

Break the captive's fet-
ters,
Light on blindness pour;
All our ills expelling,
Every bliss implore.

Show thyself a Mother;
May the Word Divine,
Born for us thine Infant,

Hear our prayers through
thine.

Virgin all excelling,
Mildest of the mild;
Freed from guilt pre-
serve us
Meek and undefiled.

Keep our lives all spot-
less,
Make our way secure,
Till we find in Jesus,
Joy for evermore.

Through the highest
heaven
To the Almighty Three,
Father, Son, and Spirit,
One same glory be.

QUEEN OF HEAVEN

QUEEN of Heaven, rejoice, alleluia:
  For He Whom you merited to bear, alleluia,
Has risen, as He said, alleluia.
Pray for us to God, alleluia.

℣. Rejoice and be glad, O Virgin Mary, alleluia.
℟. Because the Lord is truly risen, alleluia.

Let us pray. O God, Who by the Resurrection of
  Your Son,
our Lord Jesus Christ,
granted joy to the whole world:
grant, we beg You,
that through the intercession of the Virgin Mary, His
  Mother,
we may lay hold of the joys of eternal life.
Through the same Christ our Lord.

MOTHER BENIGN OF
OUR REDEEMING LORD

MOTHER benign of our redeeming Lord,
  Star of the sea and portal of the skies,
Unto your fallen people help afford—
Fallen, but striving still anew to rise.

You who did once, while wondering worlds adored,
Bear your Creator, Virgin then as now,
O by your holy joy at Gabriel's word,
Pity the sinners who before you bow.

HAIL, HOLY QUEEN

HAIL, holy Queen, Mother of mercy;
  hail, our life, our sweetness, and our hope.
To you do we cry,
poor banished children of Eve.
To you do we send up our sighs,
mourning and weeping in this valley of tears.
Turn then, most gracious Advocate,
your eyes of mercy toward us.

And after this our exile
show unto us the blessed fruit of your womb, Jesus.
O clement, O loving, O sweet Virgin Mary.

HAIL, O QUEEN OF
HEAVEN ENTHRONED

HAIL, O Queen of heaven enthroned!
Hail, by Angels Mistress owned!
Root of Jesse, Gate of morn,
Whence the world's true Light was born:

Glorious Virgin, joy to you,
Loveliest whom in heaven they view:
Fairest where all are fair,
Plead with Christ our sins to spare.

AT THE CROSS HER STATION KEEPING

AT the Cross her sta-
tion keeping,
Stood the mournful
Mother weeping,
Close to Jesus to the
last.

Through her heart, His
sorrow sharing,
All His bitter anguish
bearing,
Lo, the piercing sword
has passed!

O, how sad and sore dis-
tressed
Was that Mother highly
blessed
Of the sole-begotten One.

Christ above in torment
hangs,

She beneath beholds the
pangs
Of her dying glorious
Son.

Is there one who would
not weep
'Whelmed in miseries so
deep
Christ's dear Mother to
behold?

Can the human heart
refrain
From partaking in the
pain,
In that Mother's pain
untold?

Bruised, derided, cursed,
defiled,
She beheld her tender
Child,

All with bloody scourges rent.

For the sins of His own nation
Saw Him hang in desolation
Till His Spirit forth He sent.

O sweet Mother! fount of love,
Touch my spirit from above,
Make my heart with yours accord.

Make me feel as you have felt,
Make my soul to glow and melt
With the love of Christ, my Lord.

Holy Mother, pierce me through.
In my heart each wound renew
Of my Savior crucified.

Let me share with you His pain,
Who for all our sins was slain,
Who for me in torments died.

Let me mingle tears with you,
Mourning Him Who mourned for me,
All the days that I may live.

By the Cross with you to stay,
There with you to weep and pray,
Is all I ask of you to give.

Virgin of all virgins blest!
Listen to my fond request:
Let me share your grief Divine.

Let me, to my latest breath,
In my body bear the death
Of your dying Son Divine.

Wounded with His every wound,
Steep my soul till it has swooned
In His very Blood away.

Be to me, O Virgin, nigh,
Lest in flames I burn and die,
In His awe-full judgment day.

Christ, when You shall call me hence,
Be Your Mother my defense,
Be Your Cross my victory.

While my body here decays,
May my soul Your goodness praise,
Safe in heaven eternally.
Amen. Alleluia.

LITANY OF THE BLESSED VIRGIN MARY

LORD, have mercy
Christ have mercy.
Lord, have mercy.
Christ, hear us.
Christ, graciously hear us.
God, the Father of heaven, *have mercy on us.*
God the Son, Redeemer of the world,
have mercy on us.
God, the Holy Spirit,
have mercy on us.
Holy Trinity, one God,
have mercy on us.
Holy Mary, *pray for us.**
Holy Mother of God,
Holy Virgin of virgins,
Mother of Christ,
Mother of the Church,
Mother of Divine grace,
Mother most pure,
Mother most chaste,
Mother inviolate,
Mother undefiled,
Mother most amiable,
Mother most admirable,
Mother of good counsel,
Mother of our Creator,
Mother of our Savior,
Virgin most prudent,
Virgin most venerable,
Virgin most renowned,
Virgin most powerful,
Virgin most merciful,
Virgin most faithful,
Mirror of justice,
Seat of wisdom,
Cause of our joy,
Spiritual vessel,
Vessel of honor,
Singular vessel of devotion,
Mystical rose,
Tower of David,
Tower of ivory,
House of gold,
Ark of the covenant,
Gate of heaven,
Morning star,
Health of the sick,
Refuge of sinners,
Comforter of the afflicted,
Help of Christians,
Queen of angels,
Queen of patriarchs,
Queen of prophets,
Queen of apostles,
Queen of martyrs,
Queen of confessors,
Queen of virgins,
Queen of all saints,
Queen conceived without original sin,
Queen assumed into heaven,
Queen of the most holy Rosary,
Queen of families,
Queen of peace,

* *Pray for us* is repeated after each invocation.

Lamb of God, You take away the sins of the world; *spare us, O Lord!*

Lamb of God, You take away the sins of the world; *graciously hear us, O Lord!*

Lamb of God, You take away the sins of the world; *have mercy on us.*

℣. Pray for us, O holy Mother of God.

℟. *That we may be made worthy of the promises of Christ.*

L ET us pray.
Grant, we beg You, O Lord God,
that we Your servants
may enjoy lasting health of mind and body,
and by the glorious intercession
of the Blessed Mary, ever Virgin,
be delivered from present sorrow
and enter into the joy of eternal happiness.
Through Christ our Lord.

℟. Amen.

THE ROSARY

The devotion of the Rosary has been treasured in the Church for centuries. It is a summary of Christian faith in language and prayers inspired by the Bible. It calls to mind the most important events in the lives of Jesus and Mary. These events are called Mysteries and are divided into four groups of decades. They are: the five Joyful, the five Luminous, the five Sorrowful, and the five Glorious Mysteries. Each decade consists of one "Our Father," ten "Hail Marys," and one "Glory Be to the Father."

HOW TO SAY THE ROSARY

1. *Begin on the crucifix and say the Apostles' Creed.*
2. *On the 1st bead, say 1 Our Father.*
3. *On the next 3 beads, say Hail Mary.*
4. *Next say 1 Glory Be. Then announce and think of the first Mystery and say 1 Our Father.*
5. *Say 10 Hail Marys and 1 Glory Be to the Father.*
6. *Announce the second Mystery and continue in the same way until each of the five Mysteries of the selected group of decades is said.*

THE FIVE JOYFUL MYSTERIES

(Said on Mondays and Saturdays [except during Lent], and the Sundays from Advent to Lent)

The Joyful Mysteries direct our mind to the Son of God, Jesus Christ, our Lord and Savior, who took human nature from a human mother, Mary. They also bring to our attention some of the extraordinary events that preceded, accompanied, and followed Christ's birth.

1. The Annunciation

Lk 1:26-38; Is 7:10-15

MARY, you received with deep humility the news of the Angel Gabriel
that you were to be the Mother of God's Son;
obtain for me a similar *humility.*

2. The Visitation
Lk 1:41-50

MARY, you showed true charity in visiting Elizabeth
and remaining with her for three months
before the birth of John the Baptist;
obtain for me the grace to *love my neighbor.*

3. The Birth of Jesus
Lk 2:1-14; Mt 2:1-14; Gal 4:1-7

JESUS, You lovingly accepted poverty
when You were placed in the manger in
the stable
although You were our God and Redeemer;
grant that I may have the *spirit of poverty.*

4. The Presentation in the Temple
Lk 22:22-40

MARY, you obeyed the law of God
in presenting the Child Jesus in the
Temple;
obtain for me the *virtue of obedience.*

5. The Finding in the Temple
Lk 2:42-52

MARY, you were filled with sorrow at the
loss of Jesus
and overwhelmed with joy on finding Him
surrounded by Teachers in the Temple;
obtain for me the *virtue of piety.*

THE FIVE LUMINOUS MYSTERIES*

(Said on Thursdays [except during Lent])

The Luminous Mysteries recall to our mind important events of the Public Ministry of Christ through which He announces the coming of the Kingdom of God, bears witness to it in His works, and proclaims its demands—showing that the Mystery of Christ is most evidently a Mystery of Light.

1. Christ's Baptism in the Jordan

Mt 3:13-17; Is 42:1-2, 4-5

JESUS, at Your Baptism in the Jordan,
the Father called You His beloved Son
and the Holy Spirit descended upon You
to invest You with Your mission;
help me to keep *my Baptismal Promises.*

2. Christ's Self-Manifestation at the Wedding in Cana

Jn 2:1-11

MARY, the first among believers in Christ,
as a result of your intercession at Cana,
your Son changed water into wine
and opened the hearts of the disciples to faith;
help me to *do whatever Jesus says.*

---

* Added to the Mysteries of the Rosary by Pope John Paul II in his Apostolic Letter of October 16, 2002, entitled *The Rosary of the Virgin Mary.* They are reprinted here from our book *Pray the Rosary,* which in 2002 received the Imprimatur from Most Rev. Frank J. Rodimer, Bishop of Paterson.

3. Christ's Proclamation of the Kingdom of God

Mk 1:15; Mt 5:1-11

JESUS, You preached the Kingdom of God with its call to forgiveness,

inaugurating the ministry of mercy,

which You continue to exercise,

especially through the Sacrament of Reconciliation;

help me to *seek forgiveness for my sins.*

4. The Transfiguration of Our Lord

Mt 17:1-8; Mk 9:2-8; Lk 9:26-38

JESUS, at Your Transfiguration,
the glory of the Godhead shone forth from Your face

as the Father commanded the Apostles to hear You

and be transfigured by the Holy Spirit;

help me to *be a new person in You.*

5. Christ's Institution of the Eucharist

Mt 26:26-30; 1 Cor 11:23-25

JESUS, at the Last Supper, You instituted the Eucharist,

offering Your Body and Blood as food

under the signs of bread and wine

and testifying to Your love for humanity;

help me to attain *active participation at Mass.*

THE FIVE SORROWFUL MYSTERIES

*(Said on Tuesdays and Fridays throughout the
year, and daily from Ash Wednesday until Easter)*

*The Sorrowful Mysteries recall to our
mind the mysterious events surrounding
Christ's sacrifice of His life in order that sinful humanity might be reconciled with God.*

1. The Agony in the Garden

Mt 26:36-40

JESUS, in the Garden of Gethsemane,
You suffered a bitter agony because of
our sins;
grant me *true contrition.*

2. The Scourging at the Pillar

Mt 27:24-26; 1 Pt 2:21-25

JESUS, You endured a cruel scourging
and Your flesh was torn by heavy blows;
help me to have the *virtue of purity.*

3. The Crowning with Thorns

Mt 26:27-31

JESUS, You patiently endured the pain
from the crown of sharp thorns
that was forced upon your head;
grant me the strength to have *moral courage.*

4. The Carrying of the Cross
Mt 27:32

JESUS, You willingly carried Your Cross
for love of Your Father and all people;
grant me the *virtue of patience.*

5. The Crucifixion
Mt 27:33-50; Jn 19:31-37

JESUS, for love of me
You endured three hours of torture on the
Cross
and gave up Your spirit;
grant me the grace of *final perseverance.*

THE FIVE GLORIOUS MYSTERIES

*(Said on Wednesdays [except during Lent], and
the Sundays from Easter to Advent)*

   *The Glorious Mysteries recall to our mind
the ratification of Christ's sacrifice for the
redemption of the world, and our sharing in
the fruits of His sacrifice.*

1. The Resurrection
Mk 16:1-7; Jn 20:19-31

JESUS, You rose from the dead in triumph
and remained for forty days with Your
disciples,
instructing and encouraging them;
increase my *faith.*

2. The Ascension
Mk 16:14-20; Acts 1:1-11

JESUS, in the presence of Mary and the
disciples
You ascended to heaven
to sit at the Father's right hand;
increase the *virtue of hope* in me.

3. The Descent of the Holy Spirit
Jn 14:23-31; Acts 2:1-11

JESUS, in fulfillment of Your promise
You sent the Holy Spirit upon Mary and
the disciples
under the form of tongues of fire;
increase my *love for God.*

4. The Assumption
Lk 1:41-50; Ps 45; Gn 3:15

MARY, by the power of God You were assumed into heaven
and united with Your Divine Son;
help me to have *true devotion to you.*

5. The Crowning of the Blessed Virgin
Rv 12:1; Jdt 13:22-25

MARY, you were crowned Queen of heav-
en by your Divine Son
to the great joy of all the Saints;
obtain *eternal happiness* for me.

PRAYER AFTER THE ROSARY

O God,
   Whose only-begotten Son,
by His Life, Death, and Resurrection,
has purchased for us the rewards of eternal
   life;
grant, we beseech You, that,
meditating upon these mysteries
of the Most Holy Rosary of the Blessed Virgin
   Mary,
we may imitate what they contain
and obtain what they promise,
through the same Christ our Lord.

REMEMBER, O MOST GRACIOUS VIRGIN MARY

REMEMBER, O most gracious Virgin
   Mary,
that never was it known
that anyone who fled to your protection,
implored your help or sought your intercession,
was left unaided.
Inspired with this confidence,
I fly to you, O Virgin of virgins, my Mother;
to you do I come,
before you I stand, sinful and sorrowful.
O Mother of the Word Incarnate,
despise not my petitions,
but in your mercy hear and answer me.